Knit Scarves!

Knit Scarves!

16 Cool Patterns to Keep You Warm

CANDI JENSEN

The mission of Storey Publishing is to serve our customers by publishing practical information that encourages personal independence in harmony with the environment.

Edited by Gwen Steege and Sarah Guare
Art direction by Lisa Clark
Cover design by Susi Oberhelman
Cover and interior photographs by Kevin Kennefick
Copyedited by Margaret Radcliffe
Illustrations by Alison Kolesar
Text design by Susi Oberhelman
Text production by Jennifer Jepson Smith
Indexed by Toby Raymond

Cover yarns: Classic Merino Wool by Patons, 100% merino wool, 3.5 oz/223 yd balls, Royal Purple/#212 and Paprika/#238; Country Garden DK by Patons, 100% merino wool, 1.75 oz/128 yd balls, Sea Green/#38; Debbie Bliss Merino DK by Halcyon Yarn, 100% merino wool, 1.75 oz/122 yd skeins, #9 (pink); Funny by Sandnes Garn, 100% polyester, 1.75 oz/99 yd balls, #9400 (green). Cover design based on patterns for Odds and Ends and Fair Isle Favorite.

Copyright © 2004 by Candi Jensen

The information in this book is true and complete to the best of our knowledge. All recommendations are made without guarantee on the part of the author or Storey Publishing. The author and publisher disclaim any liability in connection with the use of this information. For additional information please contact Storey Publishing, 210 MASS MoCA Way, North Adams, MA 01247.

Storey books are available for special premium and promotional uses and for customized editions. For further information, please call 1-800-793-9396.

Printed in the China by Elegance
10 9 8 7 6 5 4 3

Library of Congress Cataloging-in-Publication Data

Jensen, Candi.
  Knit scarves! / Candi Jensen.
    p. cm.
  Includes index.
  ISBN 1-58017-577-5 (diecut hardcover : alk. paper)
  1. Knitting—Patterns. 2. Scarves. I. Title.
TT825.J4823 2004
746.43'20432—dc22
                               2004005583

Contents

Simply Knit

For the most pleasure with the least effort, no other knitting project can quite compare with making a scarf. Scarves are amazingly easy to knit because there's no shaping. And they can be knit with an almost limitless variety of yarns in a wide choice of textures, patterns, and colors. They can be warm and cozy or elegant and glittery, perfect as a gift for someone you love or a special treat for yourself. Best of all, scarves are the height of fashion and the perfect accessory to any outfit. Remember, scarves aren't just for cold weather. Whether you wear them outside your coat or as the finishing touch to a party dress, scarves are a great way to show off your personality and go a little wild. So go ahead and buy that yarn that you've been dying to work with, or simply use leftover yarn and come up with something equally wonderful. Most scarves can be knocked out in a matter of hours, not weeks. Just think of all the praise and amazement that will be heaped on you when you present that incredible scarf you just made. No one has to know that it took you only two days on the bus to and from work!

Don't forget the little ones, either. Although all the scarves in this book are long enough for an adult, most can be made short enough for a child. Kids love scarves to keep them warm, and can't you just see some little girl strutting around in a furry scarf as a fashion statement?

Whether you're a novice or an experienced knitter, you'll find great patterns and ideas in this book, along with a bunch of helpful advice. So that you have the fun of custom-designing the perfect scarf for yourself or that special someone, I've included a section on how to create your own scarf designs. I hope these ideas will inspire you to try new, fun yarns and colors. You'll be amazed at how easy it is!

Yarn, Yarn, and More Yarn

Bumpy and nubby, hairy or smooth, sometimes it's all about the yarn. You'll find an amazing array of yarn on the market these days, and when you're making a scarf, you can choose almost anything that appeals to you. Unlike a garment that has to be shaped to fit a particular person, the scarf is just a basic rectangle, with a few variations. This gives you the latitude to go wild with the most fantastic yarn. In fact, depending on the pattern you pick, the wilder the better. Fat yarn, skinny yarn, or in between, try mixing a few different ones to come up with your own effects. Combine a skinny, shiny yarn with a bumpy one or a solid-color mohair with a variegated one. Try knitting the patterns on pages 20 and 24 to get started, then feel free to experiment and come up with your own take on a novelty yarn.

When you go in search of that perfect yarn, keep in mind the person who will be wearing it, whether it's you or someone else. Yarns vary greatly in the way they feel to the touch. If you're making a scarf to wrap around your neck, hold up the yarn to your skin to see if it's comfortable and not itchy. On the other hand, if you're making a glitzy little scarf that is

more like a necklace or other accessory, then feel may not matter as much.

You should also think about how much yarn you will need and get enough at the time you purchase it. Yarn dye lots can vary greatly, and you don't want your scarf to have a sudden color shift, the sure result of a change in dye lot. Although this may not be so obvious with many of the highly textured, multicolored yarns, it's still a good idea to get enough of each yarn in the beginning. Nothing is worse than settling down to knit on a rainy evening with lots of chocolate and an old movie, then running out of yarn before the movie's over and the chocolates are gone! Besides, most yarn stores will take back unused balls of yarn for store credit, which you can use to get yarn for your next scarf.

As you leaf through this book and notice the different yarns and patterns, keep in mind that sometimes manufacturers discontinue par-ticular yarns and one or more of the yarns illustrated here may not be available anymore. We try really hard to make sure yarns will be available when the book is in your hands, but sometimes it's beyond our control. In that case, I suggest contacting the manufacturer to see what it recommends to replace it. Or your yarn store may have ideas for you.

LET'S BAG IT!

You don't need to purchase all of your knitting gear at once. But a well-supplied knitting bag, like all tool kits, makes life easier in many ways. For the scarves in this book you'll need the following, depending on the project:

- **Sets of needles, straight and circular (for knitting scarves lengthwise)**
- **Crochet hooks in small, medium, and large sizes, for picking up dropped stitches and finishing some edges**
- **6-inch metal ruler with a needle gauge (a line of graduated holes that measure the needle diameter)**
- **Retractable tape measure**
- **Rubber covers or small corks to protect your needle points and to keep the stitches from falling off when you're not knitting**
- **Assortment of blunt tapestry needles**
- **T-shaped pins**
- **Small, sharp scissors**
- **Stitch markers, both round and split**
- **Removable adhesive notepads for marking your place in directions**
- **Cable needles**
- **A nice knitting bag!**

Some Yarns Don't Mix

When you're choosing yarns to combine in the same scarf, stick to fibers that can be washed in the same manner. If you mix an acrylic that needs the heat of the dryer to put it back into shape with a mohair that shouldn't go near the heat, you will end up with a bit of a mess. Check the yarn labels for care instructions to determine whether you can mix them.

Getting Down to Basics

If you're a beginner, you'll find this section particularly helpful, and if you're a more experienced knitter, it's always good to have the reference material close at hand. Since this isn't a "how-to-knit" book, I haven't gone into great detail in this section, but I've tried to give just enough information so that you can refresh your memory.

NEEDLING AROUND

When it comes to choosing wooden, plastic, or metal needles, most knitters find that they have a preference for the type needle that works best for them. You might even find that you like a certain type of needle for each specific type of knitting. For instance, I prefer bamboo straight needles most of the time, but I find that metal ones work best for mohair and other hairy yarns. Just play around until you find what suits your own needs and tastes.

For most of the scarves in this book and, in fact, scarves in general, a pair of straight needles works fine. If you're knitting a scarf lengthwise rather than back and forth widthwise (for an example, see page 46), you'll probably find that a circular needle is easier to manage. Circular needles consist of a pair of short straight needles joined by a flexible nylon or plastic center of varying length. When you're working with a large number of stitches, you can work back and forth on them, just as you would on straight needles. Circular needles are also used when you work "in the round" in order to create a seamless tube, but none of the scarves in this book is knit circularly.

A Number of Numbers

Knitting needles come in numbered sizes, with the US, UK, and metric systems all using a different range of numbers. How's that for confusion! Luckily, most needles have both US and metric equivalents on them. If you have a pattern that indicates using UK needles, just use this handy chart for the conversions.

US	Metric	Old UK
0	2mm	14
1	2.25mm	13
	2.5mm	
2	2.75mm	12
	3mm	11
3	3.25mm	10
4	3.5mm	
5	3.75mm	9
6	4mm	8
7	4.5mm	7
8	5mm	6
9	5.5mm	5
10	6mm	4
10½	6.5mm	3
	7mm	2
	7.5mm	1
11	8mm	0
13	9mm	00
15	10mm	000

KNIT SPEAK

Yes, it is a different language, but once you learn it, unfortunately, you won't be able to use it toward that graduate degree. It's useful only for knitting patterns — and the occasional comic who thinks it's funny to read a pattern out loud. However, once you learn the abbreviations, "knit speak" will come naturally to you and you won't think twice about it. It's always helpful to have a reference chart like this, though, even if, like me, you've been knitting for years. I refer to it more than you might imagine.

cc	contrasting color
inc	increase/increasing
K	knit
K2tog	knit two stitches together
M1	make one
mc	main color
P	purl
P2tog	purl two stitches together
psso	pass slip stitch over
ssk	slip, slip, knit the two slipped stitches together
st(s)	stitch(es)
YO	yarn over

GAUGE IS ESSENTIAL

Even though you may have heard it a million times, I must stress that getting the gauge right really is the most important key to having your project turn out well. Gauge is the reference used in all patterns. If you don't come up with the same gauge as the one indicated by the pattern directions, then you won't get the right size finished project. You may think it doesn't matter with a scarf, but trust me — it does. Certainly it isn't as critical as it is for a project where you have shaping that needs to fit a body, but imagine your horror if you go to all that work making the scarf and it ends up big enough for an elephant or, equally dismaying, small enough for a doll. Just sit down and do it!

You should always measure your gauge over at least 4 inches, bigger if you need to make a particular color or stitch repeat. That's right, you also have to make your gauge swatch in the project pattern stitch or stitches. If you make an itsy-bitsy little swatch, it's hard to get an accurate measurement, especially if the recommended stitches per inch are fractional. For instance, if the gauge is 4½ stitches per inch, it's much easier to measure accurately if you can count 18 stitches over 4 inches. Here's how to measure your gauge:

1. Refer to the beginning of your pattern to see how many stitches are in 4 inches. For example, let's say the directions indicate a gauge of 16 stitches = 4" on US #7 needles. Using size 7 needles, cast on 20 stitches (the 16 plus a few edge stitches for more accurate measuring). Work using the project pattern stitch for about 5 inches (giving you a bit extra at top and bottom), then cast off. Don't block.

2. Lay the swatch on a flat, firm surface, taking care not to stretch it. Lay a flat ruler from one side of the swatch to the other and count the number of stitches within 4 inches.

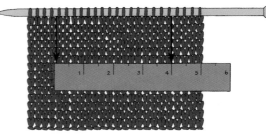

Measuring your gauge

Checking In

Even if you establish the right gauge before you begin, it's helpful to check again when you're working on the project. Sometimes you knit more tightly or loosely once the project's under way.

3. *If your swatch has more* than 16 stitches in the 4 inches, use a larger needle and knit another swatch repeating steps 1 and 2. *If your swatch contains fewer* than the 16 stitches in the 4 inches, use smaller needles and repeat the swatch process. Always use fresh yarn when you make a swatch, as used yarn has often stretched and won't give you an accurate measurement.

Casting On

When I first learned to knit, at age 8, I just put loops on the needle and then knit into them. For those of you who are still putting loops on the needle, I can attest that there is a much

Loosen Up!

If you tend to cast on too tightly, use a needle size one step larger for casting on and then work your first and subsequent rows with the correct-size needle.

better way to do it! It wasn't until I was knitting cute little things for my first baby that I found a much stronger and more even way to cast on. Casting on with the following method will give you a neat, firm but elastic edge, so much better than the loops.

1. Estimate how long to make the "tail" by wrapping the yarn around the needle one time for each cast-on stitch you need, then adding a few extra inches. Make a slip knot right here and slide the knot over a single knitting needle. Hold that needle in your right hand; hold the tail and the working end of the yarn in your left hand as shown. Insert the needle through the front loop of the tail on your thumb. Bring the needle tip over and behind the working yarn on your finger.

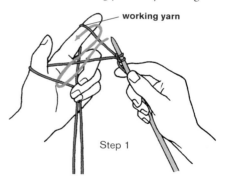

Step 1

2. Use the needle to draw the working yarn through the tail loop on your thumb.

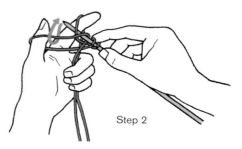

Step 2

3. Release the tail loop on your thumb, place your thumb underneath the tail, and pull both yarns to tighten while holding both firmly against your palm.

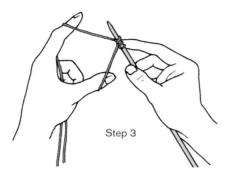

Step 3

Casting Off

Just as one might think, casting off is getting rid of stitches. Also referred to as binding off, to get to this point always brings about a great feeling, because it means you've accomplished your wonderful project. Be sure you don't cast off too tightly (unless the pattern calls for it) or the end of the scarf will be a different width from the beginning — kind of puckered, as it were. If your cast off tends to be too tight, go ahead and use a larger needle for this step.

To cast off, work two stitches, then draw the first one over the second and let it drop.

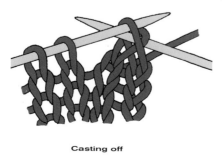

Casting off

Work the next stitch, then draw the next one over it and let it drop as before. Continue in this manner working one stitch at a time, then drawing the preceding one over it, until you reach the end of the row. When you have just one stitch left, cut the yarn, leaving about 10 inches, and draw that end through the stitch last. Pull firmly to tighten. Thread the end through a yarn needle and weave it back along the row of stitches as invisibly as possible.

Carrying a Second Color

Working a scarf with color changes has a few extra challenges, but nothing that you can't deal with. First, let's go over how to do the actual color changes.

In this book, we illustrate color sequences in charts that are color-matched to the photos of the finished projects. Follow charts starting at the bottom line and read them from right to left on knit rows and from left to right on purl rows. We've placed a "start here" arrow on the charts as a reminder. If you use a different color scheme from ours, you may want to tape yarn swatches over the printed key to keep yourself on track.

When you knit with more than one color, you'll need to carry along the color or colors you're not using on the wrong side until they're needed again. It's important to keep the carried yarn loose so that it doesn't pucker the fabric. Now with scarves, this can prove to be a bit more of a challenge since the back of the scarf will also be on display. Normally, you wouldn't

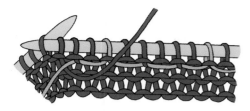

Carry being caught up every two stitches

want to carry the yarn for more than three stitches, but on a scarf it might be advisable to carry it for no more than two stitches. That way it will look better on the underside, and you won't end up with long loops that not only are unattractive but also can get caught or pulled. To catch the carried yarn, just wrap the working yarn from beneath and around it every two or three stitches, as shown above.

When changing colors, always take the color you want to emphasize from below the other (see diagram on page 73). On the front, the color handled this way will dominate the pattern and create a more uniform design. Be sure to take the same color consistently from below throughout the project.

If you are able to hold one color yarn in one hand and the second color in the other hand, you'll find that two-color knitting goes much more quickly and easily.

Yarns: Your Choice

For each scarf in the book, you can substitute any yarn that knits comfortably at the same gauge. For some scarves, we have included yarn variations.

Joining a New Yarn

You've run out of yarn! Not to worry. Here are two easy ways to join in the new yarn.

The simplest way is to lay the new yarn over the old yarn so that you can knit the two together for three or four stitches, then drop the old yarn and continue with the new. When you come to those doubled stitches in the next row, be sure to knit the two yarns together as one. Be aware that if the yarn you're using is very smooth, plain, and/or inelastic, this kind of join may show. If it is very bulky, your stitches may be noticeably larger.

A less visible method is to catch a tail of the new yarn under the old for six or seven stitches, then cut the old yarn, leaving a tail that you can catch for another six or seven stitches. This technique is similar to the one you use when you carry a second color in multicolor knitting.

DIY . . . or Design It Yourself!

You can definitely design your own scarves, even if you are a beginner. I will try to make this as straightforward and easy to follow as I can, and then all you have to do is have fun. So no excuses. Go ahead and get that really incredible yarn and make the scarf of your dreams!

To start with, you need to establish two basics: the stitch pattern you will use and the dimensions of the scarf. For your first project, let's do a garter stitch scarf that's 6 inches wide by 60 inches long. Remember that garter stitch is simply knitting every row.

The "Don't Panic" Department

Beginning knitters often panic when they drop a stitch. It's empowering to discover how easy it is to pick up dropped or half-made stitches. And this is one of the reasons you need to include a crochet hook in your knitting bag! Working on the right side of stockinette stitch, find the last loop that's still knitted and insert the crochet hook from front to back. (On the wrong side, insert the needle from back to front.) Pull the loop just above the bar between the adjacent stitches, catch the bar with your hook, and draw it through the loop. If you have to pick up a number of stitches, take care to pick up the bars in the correct order.

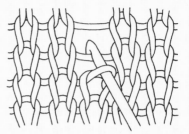

Picking up a dropped stitch knitwise

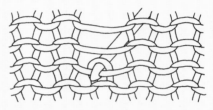

Picking up a dropped stitch purlwise

Let's assume you've found an incredible yarn. It's always a good idea to check the label on the yarn to see what the manufacturer recommends for the needle size and gauge before making your gauge swatch. So let's say the recommendation is for a US #8 needle with 16 stitches to 4 inches. Following the directions on page 10, make a garter stitch gauge swatch and see what you come up with. If you like the texture and feel of your swatch, but don't quite achieve the number of recommended stitches, it doesn't really matter. However, if the fabric feels a bit too open or lacks the amount of body you're looking for, then go down a needle size to get a denser knit. If, on the other hand, it's too stiff and won't drape nicely, as a scarf should, go up a size. Being the smarty pants that you are, you may indeed come up with 16 stitches to 4 inches after all. Now, just follow the next few steps, and voilà — you'll have a scarf pattern!

1. Calculate the number of stitches per inch by dividing the number of stitches in 4 inches by 4. For example, 16 ÷ 4" = 4 stitches per inch.

2. You want your scarf to be 6 inches wide, so multiply 6 by the number of stitches per inch you get with your yarn: 6" wide × 4 stitches per inch = 24 stitches total.

3. Cast on 24 stitches. For a 60 inch long scarf, knit in garter stitch until the scarf measures 60 inches. Cast off loosely.

Impressed with how easy that was? Now let's say you want to make a scarf that has more than one color or one with a pattern stitch. You must make your gauge swatch in the stitch desired and find out your stitches per inch just as before, but this time you need to take into account the stitch repeat of the pattern. You can invent your own stitch sequence or refer to a "stitch book." Stitch books are basically encyclopedias of stitches. These wonderful references contain dozens of stitch and color patterns that you can work into your own designs. They can also be helpful when working a pattern that you don't quite understand, because they provide all the basic stitches and techniques along with their abbreviations. I highly recommend that you have one on hand.

Stitch books usually indicate the number of stitches in each repeat. For instance, a "knit 2, purl 2" rib is a repeat of four stitches. Some stitch repeats call for an additional number of stitches beyond the main sequence: for example, "4 + 2." This simply means that the pattern consists of four stitches that are repeated across the row, completed by an additional two stitches that can be on either end to balance the design and make the pattern come out right.

For this exercise, let's work a knit 2, purl 2 rib using the same yarn you used for your first swatch. The swatch will need to have a "4 + 2" pattern stitch repeat so your rib will come out even. Go ahead and make your gauge swatch. You probably will get about 24 stitches to 4 inches. The rib pattern pulls in the stitches so you get more stitches per inch than when you work stockinette or garter stitch. Thus, in order to make a 6-inch-wide scarf, you need to cast on more stitches than for the preceding example.

Make sure the total number of stitches is evenly divisible by the pattern stitch repeat. If the number doesn't come out even, simply

How to Calculate Number of Stitches Required

Photocopy the formula below and keep it handy for easy reference. (Determine the number of stitches per inch by doing a gauge swatch. See page 10.)

For most scarves:
Width of scarf ____" × stitches per inch ____ = number of stitches required ____

For scarves with color or stitch patterns:
Stitch pattern = ____ stitches
Number of stitches required ____ ÷ number of pattern stitches ____ = ____
NOTE: If this is not a whole number, adjust the number of stitches required up or down to the closest number that is evenly divisible by the number of pattern stitches. Recalculate the scarf width as follows:
New number of stitches required ____ ÷ stitches per inch ____ = scarf width ____

Making Pompoms

These fuzzy balls can be as large or as small as you like.

1. Cut a block of cardboard that is as wide as you want your pompom to be.
2. Wrap yarn around the cardboard 50–125 times, depending on the pompom's diameter and the yarn's weight. Keep the strands evenly spaced and don't overlap them too much at the center.

Making a pompom or tassel: Step 2

3. Insert an 8-inch length of yarn through one side of the wrapped yarn. Use the yarn to gather the group of wrapped yarn together snugly, and tie tightly.

4. Slide the tip of your scissors under the yarn at the opposite edge and cut through all the layers.

Making a pompom or tassel: Steps 3 & 4

5. Remove the cardboard and trim the edges of the pompom to round and neaten it.
6. Thread the ends of the knot through a needle and use them to fasten the pompom to the scarf.

---

adjust the size of your scarf to accommodate the stitch pattern. For example, if your pattern repeat is 5 stitches and your gauge is 24 stitches to 4 inches, add another stitch to bring the total to 25. Your scarf width will be slightly more than 4 inches, but the 5-stitch pattern will repeat evenly within the 25 stitches. (For a 5-inch-wide scarf, you'd need 30 stitches.) Use the same approach when knitting a color pattern, such as in Fair Isle design.

Living on the Edge

Have a little fun with your scarf and give it a great finishing touch. Although the ubiquitous fringe is the usual ending to a scarf story, you may want to try something out of the ordinary. Think about adding pompoms (see above), as I've done to the Cable Car scarf on page 36, or beading, feathers, or fabric (see photos on facing page). Try beginning and ending a scarf

Feather fringe

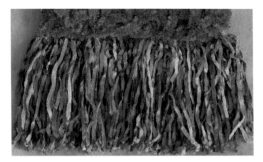

Ready-made fringe

Beaded fringe

Lace Stitch *

How to Make a Fringe

1. Cut a length of yarn twice as long as you want the finished fringe to be, plus about 2 inches.

2. Holding several strands of yarn together (some patterns indicate how many strands to use), fold the yarn in half.

3. Use a crochet hook to draw the folded loop through from the right side to the wrong side of the scarf end, going through a whole stitch (two loops) on the scarf edge.

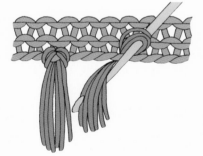

4. Thread the free ends through the loop and pull firmly to tie the fringe to the scarf edge.

with a color pattern (see page 70), or a lace stitch such as what I've done with the border of the Mohair and Lace scarf on page 50. Use your imagination and come up with something completely different.

* See page 93 for pattern.

The Final Touches

Before you can give or wear your beautiful new scarf, you'll need to weave in any loose yarn tails at the ends of the scarf or where you joined a new yarn. Thread the end that needs to be woven in through a large-eye yarn or tapestry needle. Working on the wrong side of the piece, weave the yarn in and out along the row for about 2 inches, then turn and weave it back in the direction it came from for a few more stitches, just to lock it in place. Although it may be tempting, you should never weave in more than one end of yarn at the same place, because it will be bulky and show. Also, make sure that the yarn end doesn't show on the right side of the work. Cut off any excess yarn.

It's done, you've woven in the ends, and you're dying to wear it . . . but wait, it's rolling into a large sausage. This isn't always a bad thing. A rolled scarf can actually be a more updated look. It used to be that a scarf had to be as flat as a board or you were doing something wrong, but now many fashionable scarves roll onto themselves and it's a *good* thing. If it doesn't conflict with the look you're going for, just let it roll!

On the other hand, if you want a scarf that lies flat and the pattern stitch that you used didn't prevent the roll, all isn't lost — you can block it. For wool projects, one way to block is to steam the scarf by pinning it to the size you want and holding a steam iron over it until the steam penetrates the fabric. Alternatively, you can cover the fabric surface with a wet pressing cloth and lightly touch the iron to it. With either of these techniques, take care not to press too hard or you will damage the wool and lose the lovely texture of the pattern. It's especially important not to distort cables and ribs.

For wool blends, mohair, angora, alpaca, or cashmere, just dampen the knitted piece by spraying it lightly with water, then pin it to a flat surface where you can safely leave it to air dry. Blocking a scarf knit with synthetic fibers is a whole other ballgame. Unlike wool and other natural fibers, synthetic fibers often don't respond well when treated with heat and/or steam. Blocking may cause furry or hairy yarns to become matted, so you probably should avoid blocking scarves made with these yarns. If you feel the project needs some finishing, pin the piece into the desired size and shape, spritz with water, and allow it to air dry. Although this technique may not be as effective as blocking natural fibers, it does provide some shaping. Always check the yarn label for care instructions for guidance in how to treat the specific yarn you're working with.

Flat as a Pancake

To avoid the rolled-edge look, choose a project that features a pattern stitch that you work throughout the length of the scarf, such as seed, moss, or slip stitch.

A Touch of Fur

This soft, fuzzy scarf is knit entirely with garter stitch. Non-knitters will never guess how truly easy it is to make. You just knit every row! The fabric looks the same on both sides, and most garter stitch scarves won't roll along the edges. The stitch is perfect for all types of yarn, thick or thin, furry or smooth, colorful or plain. And the look is completely different, depending on the yarn you choose. On page 23 you'll find garter stitch swatches knit with different yarns. Can you believe they all are knit following exactly the same pattern? Garter stitch scarves are great projects for beginning knitters!

Finished measurements

4" x 60"

Yarn

Scarf on left: The Great Adirondack Yarn Co., 100% rayon, 3.75 oz (100g)/85 yd (78m) skeins

1 skein Wildflowers/#1223

Scarf on right: Fun Fur by Lion Brand Yarn, 60% cotton/40% microfiber, 1.75 oz (50g)/98 yd (90m) balls

2 balls Lava/#204

Needles

One pair US #11 (8mm) straight needles, *or size you need to obtain gauge*

Gauge

12 sts = 4" in garter stitch (knit every row). *Please take time to check your gauge.*

Other supplies

Large-eye yarn needle for weaving in ends

KNITTING THE SCARF	
SET UP	Cast on 12 stitches.
Row 1	Knit to end of row.
Next Rows	Knit to end of each row until the scarf measures 60 inches, or desired length.
FINISHING	
	Cast off all stitches loosely. Use a large-eye yarn needle to weave in all ends.

Some Basic Tips

Cast on loosely. It is important that your cast-on stitches aren't too tight, or you'll have trouble working your first row. Worse, a too-tight cast-on row also causes the edge on the finished project to draw in. If you're having trouble loosening up, here are some tips that may help:

- Cast on to two needles held together, then remove one needle.
- Try not to pull your stitches too close together as you work.
- For the cast-on, use a slightly larger needle than what is called for, then switch to the correct size when you begin knitting.

Keep count. Take time to count the number of stitches you have every few rows. Especially when you're working with textured novelty yarns, it's easy to gain or lose a stitch, and you'll want to fix your mistake early on!

Weave in ends. It is important to weave in yarn ends when changing colors or when you need to begin a new ball of yarn, in order to create a smooth and attractive scarf. (Refer to page 13 for adding new yarn.) Here are some suggestions for making your tail ends as invisible as possible:

- Be sure to weave in the ends *along* the rows widthwise (not length-wise). After weaving four or five stitches, reverse directions and weave back the way you came for two or three stitches. This should tightly lock in the end.
- Try to make your changes at the ends rather than in the middle of the row so that you can weave in tails close to the edge of the scarf, where they'll be less noticeable.

Other Yarns to Try

Swatch 1: La Gran by Classic Elite, 77% mohair/17% wool/6% nylon, 1.5 oz /90 yd balls, #6577

Swatch 2: Optik by Berroco, 48% cotton/21% acrylic/20% mohair/8% metallic/ 3% polyester, 1.75 oz/87 yd skeins, Van Gogh/#4923

Swatch 3: Zoom by Classic Elite, 50% alpaca/50% wool, 1.75 oz/52 yd balls, White/#016

Odds & Ends

This scarf is perfect for using up odd bits of yarn that are lying around. As long as you can get close to the same gauge with each of the various yarns, it will work fine. If you want to use a finer yarn than the others, try doubling it or using it together with another fine yarn. The more random you make the changes, the better, so don't feel you have to have the same number of rows for each yarn. I've listed the yarns I used in the scarf shown here, but you can use others, and as many as you like. Have fun with it!

Finished measurements

4" x 78"

Yarns

Lavish by Berroco, 40% nylon/32% wool/ 15% polyester/13% acrylic, 1.75 oz (50g)/ 55 yd (50m) balls

    1 ball Cadaquez/#7334

Matchmaker DK by Jaeger, 100% merino wool, 1.75 oz (50g)/131 yd (120m) balls

    1 ball #887 (bright pink)

Quest by Berroco, 100% nylon, 1.75 oz (50g)/ 82 yd (76m) skeins

    1 skein Marilyn Pink/#9831

Needles

One pair US #10 (6mm) straight needles, *or size you need to obtain gauge*

Gauge

16 stitches = 4" in garter stitch (knit every row). *Please take time to check your gauge.*

Other supplies

Large-eye yarn needle for weaving in ends

KNITTING THE SCARF	
Set up	Cast on 16 stitches.
Row 1	Knit to end of row.
Next Rows	Knit to end of each row, changing yarns randomly, as desired, until the scarf measures 78 inches, or desired length.
FINISHING	
	Cast off all stitches loosely. Use a large-eye yarn needle to weave in all ends.

Handling Three Colors

You may carry the colors up the side instead of cutting them when not in use. Be sure to bring the new active yarn from *beneath* the other colors.

If you choose to cut the old color yarns instead, leave a tail of 6 to 8 inches (15 to 20cm). Knit the first stitch with the new color, leaving another tail of the same length. Hold the two tails fairly tightly between the third and fourth fingers of your right hand.

On the next knit stitch, maintain tension on the two tails and twist them around the working yarn just before you knit the stitch. Do this for five or six stitches.

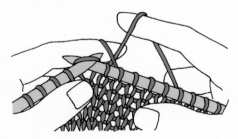

Carrying new yarn along the back

Carried yarn on back

Other Yarns to Try

Swatch 1: Cotton Classic by Tahki/Stacy Charles, 100% mercerized cotton, 1.75 oz/108 yd skeins, #3476 and #3003; Imagine by Classic Elite, 53% cotton/47% rayon, 1.6 oz/93 yd skeins, #9207

Swatch 2: Twister by Patons, 65% polyester/35% acrylic, 1.75 oz/47 yd balls, Bongo Blues/#05735; Karisma by Garnstudio, 100% superwash wool, 1.75 oz/ 100 yd skeins, Peacock Blue/#27; Cotton Chenille Yarn by Crystal Palace, 100% mercerized cotton, 1.75 oz/98 yd skeins, Periwinkle/#1404

Swatch 3: India Ribbon Yarn by Lana Grossa, 100% microfiber nylon, 1.6 oz/60 yd balls, #07; ¼" Sparkle Ribbon by Prism, 95% rayon/5% lurex, 2.5 oz/90 yd skeins, Ginger; Zen by Berroco, 60% nylon/40% cotton, 1.75 oz/ 110 yd skeins, Hijiki Green/#8227

Classic Stripes

Easy stripes in a wide rib pattern make this scarf a classic.
It is made in luscious soft alpaca that is just begging to be wrapped
around your neck — or his. The classic look and soft hand make
it a perfect "guy" scarf. It is worked with two strands of yarn
held together so it will work up fast and be toasty warm.

Finished measurements

5½" x 57"

Yarns

Inca Alpaca by Classic Elite, 100% alpaca,
1.75 oz (50g)/109 yd (97m) balls

    2 skeins mc   # 1120 (light teal)
    1 skein cc A   #1146 (dark teal)
    1 skein cc B   #1197 (bright green)

Needles

One pair US #10 (6mm) straight needles, *or
size you need to obtain gauge*

Gauge

16 stitches = 4", 14 rows = 4" in Rib Stitch
pattern (see page 30). *Please take time
to check your gauge.*

Other supplies

Large-eye yarn needle for weaving in ends

---

cc = contrasting color ◆ **mc** = main
color

KNITTING THE SCARF

NOTE	Rows 1 and 2 are the Rib Stitch pattern. Continue to work in this pattern stitch throughout the scarf while at the same time changing colors to create the stripes. It would be helpful to try weaving in your color change ends as you work.
SET UP	Working with two strands of cc B yarn held together, cast on 26 stitches.
Row 1	*Purl 2, knit 6; repeat from * to the last 2 stitches; purl 2.
Row 2	*Knit 2, purl 6; repeat from * to the last 2 stitches; knit 2.
Rows 3–12	Repeat Rows 1 and 2 (Rib Stitch pattern).
Rows 13–26	Change to mc and continue to work Rib Stitch pattern.
Rows 27–28	Change to cc A and continue to work Rib Stitch pattern.
Rows 29–30	Change to mc and continue to work Rib Stitch pattern.
Rows 31–34	Change to cc A and continue to work Rib Stitch pattern.
Next Rows	Repeat Rows 13–34 nine more times.
Next 14 Rows	Change to mc and continue to work Rib Stitch pattern.
Next 12 Rows	Change to cc B and continue to work Rib Stitch pattern.

FINISHING

	Cast off all stitches loosely. With a large-eye yarn needle, weave in ends.
NOTE	If the scarf rolls at the edges and you want it to lay flat, see page 18 for blocking instructions.

"Tweedy" Stripe

Don't be afraid to try different yarns with the stripe pattern on page 29, or even to try different stripe widths. Stripe patterns are especially fun to work with because by making minor changes, you can create an entirely new look!

At the right I show a couple of ways to alter the classic stripe and give the scarf a little pizzazz. The tweedy effect is created by working two different-colored yarns at the same time. When knitting the stripe, hold one strand of your main yarn and one strand of another color. (**Tip:** To keep the different-colored yarns from tangling, you may want to put each ball in a separate plastic container — the type you might get at the deli — and cut a hole in the center of the lid for the yarn to come through.) At the bottom of the scarf I used a novelty fur yarn as an edging for about 3 inches, which really jazzes it up!

In this pattern, you can also vary the width of the ribs. For instance, knit 4, purl 4 for an even rib or knit 8, purl 2 for even wider "stockinette" panels. Feel free to experiment with all of the patterns in this book. Scarf knitting may be simple, but it can be fun and creative, too. See pages 13–17 for advice on how to DIY ("design it yourself").

Other Yarns to Try

Bazic Wool by Classic Elite, 100% superwash wool, 1.75 oz/65 yd balls, #2916 and #2976

Mustacio by Friends, 100% acrylic, 3.5 oz/150 yd skeins, Burgundy/#03

Chunky Monkey

Make it quick, make it big! Thick chunky yarns that work up in a jiffy are all the rage. This scarf is worked in an easy "mock" rib stitch that allows you to knit 1, purl 1 only every other row — we love that. Brilliantly colored print yarn will brighten up a cold, dreary day and keep you snuggly warm at the same time.

Finished measurements
6" x 76" (not including fringe)

Yarn
Biggy Print by Rowan, 100% wool, 3.5 oz (100g)/33 yd (30m) balls

    4 balls Fiesta/#251

Needles
One pair US #15 (10mm) needles, *or size you need to obtain gauge*

Gauge
8 sts = 4" in Mock Rib Stitch pattern (see page 34). *Please take time to check your gauge.*

Other supplies
Large eye-yarn needle for weaving in ends

	KNITTING THE SCARF
NOTE	This scarf is knit entirely in the Mock Rib Stitch pattern (see Rows 1 and 2 below).
SET UP	Cast on 13 stitches.
Row 1	*Purl 1, knit 1; repeat from * to end of row; purl 1.
Row 2	Knit to end of row.
Next Rows	Repeat Rows 1 and 2 until scarf measures 76 inches, or desired length.
	Cast off all stitches loosely.
	FINISHING
	With large-eye yarn needle, weave in all loose ends.
	Make 16 fringes 8½ inches long and attach 8 at each end of the scarf. (For instructions on making and attaching fringe, see page 17.)
	If the scarf edges roll and you want them to lie flat, follow the instructions for blocking on page 18.

It's All About Embellishment

A flower here, a little embroidery there — it's really endless what originality you can add to your scarves. Take that plain scarf and make a real statement of it by adding a few personal touches. If you feel brave, make a ribbon flower on your own or simply buy a few ready-made and sew them on. For a little monogramming action, embroider your initials, or maybe a trailing vine with some grapes on it. Or why not try a little beading?

Other Yarns to Try

Swatch 1: Big Wool by Rowan, 100% merino wool, 3.5 oz/87 yd balls, Pip/#015

Swatch 2: Kid Classic by Rowan (2 strands held together), 70% lamb's wool/26% kid mohair/4% nylon, 1.75 oz/153 yd balls, Pinched/#819

Swatch 3: Bulky Rayon Chenille by Blue Heron Yarns, 100% rayon, 8 oz/275 yd skeins, Tulip

Cable Car

Don't you just love a classic white cable scarf? It's so versatile that you can wear it either to a football game or to dinner and a movie. Made with an "angora" blend yarn that is extra toasty (ever see a cold bunny running around?), it will make you smile as it moves through your fingers. Cables do take some extra time, but the results are well worth it!

Finished measurements

7.25" x 72"

Yarn

Lush by Classic Elite, 50% angora/50% wool, 3.5 oz (100g)/223 yd (205m) balls

    4 skeins #4416 (off-white)

Needles

One pair US #9 (5.5mm) needles, *or size you need to obtain gauge*

Gauge

23 sts = 4" in cable stitch patterns (see page 38).

    Please take time to check your gauge.

Other supplies

Large-eye yarn needle for weaving in ends, bulky cable needle

Cable Stitches

Corded Cable (6 stitches)

Rows 1 and 3: Knit 6.

Rows 2, 4, and 6: Purl 6.

Row 5: Slip 3 stitches onto the cable needle. Hold cable needle at back of work. Knit 3 from the main needle, then knit the 3 stitches from the cable needle.

Corded Cable

Braided Cable (14 stitches)

Rows 1 and 3: *Knit 2, purl 2; repeat from * to the last 2 stitches; knit 2.

Rows 2 and 4: *Purl 2, knit 2; repeat from * to the last 2 stitches; purl 2.

Row 5: *Slip 4 stitches onto the cable needle. Holding the cable needle at front of work, knit 2 from the left needle. Slip the 2 purl stitches from the cable needle to the left needle and purl these 2 stitches. Knit 2 from the cable needle; repeat from *. Purl 2.

Rows 6, 8, and 10: *Purl 2, knit 2; repeat from * to last 2 stitches; purl 2.

Rows 7 and 9: *Knit 2, purl 2; repeat from * to last 2 stitches; knit 2.

Row 11: Knit 2, purl 2, slip 4 stitches onto the cable needle. Holding the cable needle at back of work, knit 2 from the left needle. Slip the 2 purl stitches from the cable needle to the left needle and purl these 2 stitches. Knit 2 from the cable needle. Purl 2, knit 2.

Row 12: *Purl 2, knit 2; repeat from * to last 2 stitches; purl 2.

Braided Cable

KNITTING THE SCARF	
NOTE	For Corded Cable and Braided Cable Stitch patterns, see facing page. Notice that the first and last two stitches form a textured edging that also helps keep the scarf edge from rolling when worn. To help you keep track of where the cables begin and end, place stitch markers on both sides of each one.
SET UP	With US #9 needles, cast on 46 stitches.
Row 1	Knit 2, purl 3, work Corded Cable Stitch, purl 5, work Braided Cable Stitch, purl 5, work Corded Cable Stitch, purl 3, knit 2.
Row 2	Knit 5, work Corded Cable Stitch, knit 5, work Braided Cable Stitch, knit 5, work Corded Cable Stitch, knit 5.
Next Rows	Repeat Rows 1 and 2, working the 6-row repeat of the Corded Cable Stitch and the 12-row repeat of the Braided Cable Stitch as established until the piece measures 70". Continue working in pattern until you complete Row 9 of the Braided Cable Stitch.
	Cast off all stitches loosely in pattern (knitting the knit stitches and purling the purl stitches).
FINISHING	
	With large-eye yarn needle, weave in ends.
	Following the directions on page 16, make 10 pompoms, each 2" in diameter. Sew five evenly spaced on the edge at each end of the scarf.

Working a Cable

To make a cable, place the number of stitches specified in the pattern on a third needle and hold them either behind or in front of the knitted piece, as directed. Work the next stitches on your left-hand needle according to the pattern, then work the stitches from the cable needle. Take care not to twist the stitches.

Garden of Flowers

It's always a pleasure to see a flower garden in the middle of winter, so if you don't have one outside your window, you can wrap one around your neck! Worked in a simple seed stitch, the scarf is wonderful on its own, but adding the ribbon flowers will bring it up a notch to extra special. The flowers are easy to make and can be completed by a beginner.

Finished measurements

10" x 60"

Yarn

Aristocrat by Heirloom, 50% mohair/50% wool, 1.75 oz (50g)/83 yd (76m) balls

    3 balls Burgundy/#328

Needles

One pair US #10 (6mm) needles, *or size you need to obtain gauge*

Gauge

14 stitches = 4" in Seed Stitch pattern (see page 42). *Please take time to check your gauge.*

Other supplies

Large-eye yarn needle for weaving in ends, 2 yards wired ribbon, sewing needle, and thread to match yarn

KNITTING THE SCARF	
NOTE	This scarf is knit completely in Seed Stitch pattern (knit 1, purl 1 to end of row every row). Seed stitch is worked on an odd number of stitches, which means you always knit into the purl stitches and purl into the knit stitches. The finished look is nicely textured.
SET UP	Cast on 35 stitches.
Row 1	*Knit 1, purl 1; repeat from * to end of row; knit 1.
Next Rows	Repeat Row 1 until scarf measures 60", or desired length.
FINISHING	
	Cast off all stitches loosely, continuing in pattern (knit 1, purl 1) as you cast off.
	Using a large-eye yarn needle, weave in all loose ends.

Another Yarn to Try

Wings by Classic Elite, 55% alpaca/23% silk/22% wool/hollow core, 1.75 oz/129 yd skeins, #2347

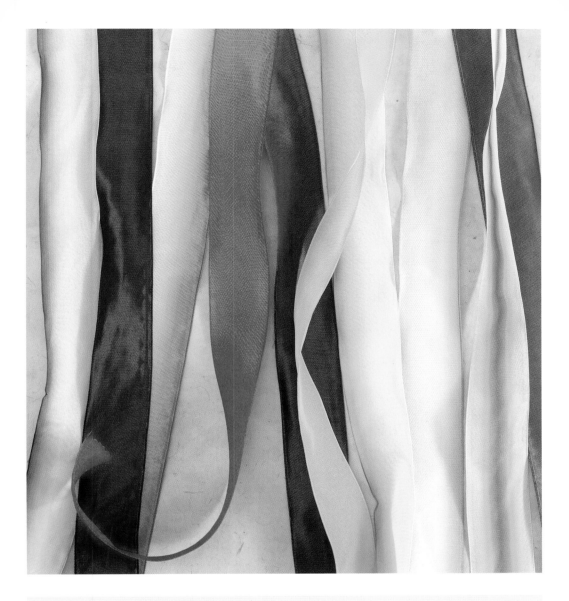

Miles of Rippling Ribbons

Wired ribbon is a beautiful material to work with. Follow the directions on the following pages to make ribbon flowers. You can experiment with different colors and patterns, or use the flowers as friendly embellishments for other projects.

Making Ribbon Flowers

Large Flower
Materials:
1 yard of 1½" wide wired ribbon,
   multicolored (half green and half
   purple)
Green sewing thread to match
   the ribbon
Sewing needle

1. With the purple side up, fold down
one end (on the diagonal) toward you,
letting the tail overlap the bottom ribbon
edge by ½".

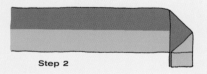

2. Then fold this portion in half (see
dotted line in Step 1). This will be
the center of the flower.

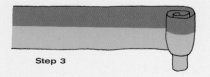

3. Now start to roll the folded end
between your thumb and finger for
two or three turns.

4. On the opposite end, take hold of the
bottom wire and start to pull it, gathering
up the ribbon as you pull until you have
gathers all the way to the part that you
are holding. Then wrap the gathered
edge around the center until you have
wrapped all of the ribbon. Cut the
excess wire and fold down the last
inch to form a triangle. With matching
thread, sew the gathered portion of the
flower in place. (Refer to the photo.)
Make sure the wire is securely tucked
in so it doesn't scratch or show.

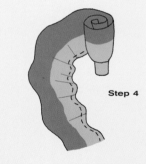

Small Flower
Materials:
18 inches of 1½" wide wired ribbon, multicolored (half green and half purple)

Purple sewing thread to match the ribbon

Sewing needle

To make the small flower, hold the ribbon with the green side up and follow the directions for the large flower. Since you are working with less ribbon, you will end up with a smaller flower.

Large Leaf
Materials:
1 yard of 1" wide green satin ribbon

Green sewing thread to match the ribbon

Sewing needle

1. Using 12" length of ribbon, fold it in half lengthwise, with right sides together. Sew one end on the diagonal beginning ½" from the end on the open edge and stitching toward the corner of the folded edge; lock stitches with a back stitch, then work a running stitch the length of the ribbon about ⅛" from the fold.

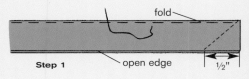

Step 1 fold open edge ½"

2. Pull the running stitch so it gathers up the ribbon. Run a diagonal line of stitch-

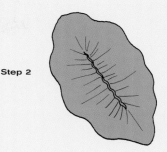

Step 2

ing at the end of the ribbon to match the opposite end. Open the leaf and attach the gathered portion to the scarf. Refer to the photo for placement.

Small Leaf
Materials:
9 inches of 1" wide green satin ribbon

Green sewing thread to match the ribbon

Sewing needle

Work as for the large leaf.

Long and Skinny

Didn't someone once say you can't be too tall or too thin? Well, I don't buy it for people, but it might work for this scarf. Only a scant 2¾" wide, this long tall Sally is worked with a bunch of stitches but very few rows. In other words, you are casting on the *length* of the scarf and not the width. The Slip Stitch pattern is easy to master, and when it is worked in stripes, it gives the scarf a woven look.

Finished measurements

2¾" x 84" (not including fringe)

Yarn

Merino Big by Lana Grossa, 100% wool,
    1.75 oz (50g)/130 yd (120m) balls

mc = 1 ball #010 (cream)

cc A = 1 ball #017 (olive)

cc B = 1 ball #028 (dark purple)

cc C = 1 ball #026 (lavender)

cc D = 1 ball #040 (dark orange)

cc E = 1 ball #038 (light orange)

Needles

One US #10½ (6.5mm) 26" circular needle,
    or size you need to obtain gauge

Gauge

19 stitches = 4" in Slip Stitch pattern (see page 48). *Please take time to check your gauge.*

Other supplies

Large-eye yarn needle for weaving in ends

---

cc = contrasting color ◆ **mc** = main color

NOTE	This scarf is worked completely in the Slip Stitch pattern that you will establish in Rows 1 and 2. At the same time that you maintain the Slip Stitch pattern, change colors as indicated in directions below. Although you work Rows 1 and 2 alternately throughout, some of the stripes contain three rows. This means that you don't always work a Row 1 at the beginning of each new color.
SET UP	Using mc, cast on 400 stitches.
Row 1	*Knit 1, move yarn to front and slip the next stitch purlwise, move yarn back; repeat from * to end of row.
Row 2	*Purl 1, move yarn to the back and slip the next stitch purlwise, move yarn to the front; repeat from * to end of row.
Rows 3 and 4	Change to cc A and repeat Rows 1 and 2.
Rows 5–8	Change to cc B and repeat Rows 1 and 2.
Rows 9 and 10	Change to cc C and repeat Rows 1 and 2.
Rows 11–13	Change to cc D and repeat Rows 1 and 2, ending with Row 1.
Row 14	Change to cc E. *Purl 1, move yarn to the back and slip the next st purlwise, move yarn to the front; repeat from * to end of row. NOTE: This is the same as Row 2.
Row 15	*Knit 1, move yarn to front and slip the next st purlwise, move yarn back; repeat from * to end of row. NOTE: This is the same as Row 1.

Slipping Purlwise

To slip a stitch purlwise, insert the right-hand needle into the front of the next stitch on the left-hand needle as if you were going to purl it, then slip it to the right-hand needle without working it.

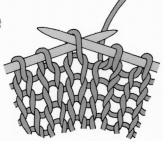

Rows 16 and 17	Change to mc and repeat Rows 14 and 15.
Rows 18 and 19	Change to cc B and repeat Rows 14 and 15.
Rows 20–22	Change to cc A and repeat Rows 14 and 15, then repeat Row 14 once more.
Row 23	Change to mc and repeat Row 15.
Rows 24–25	Change to cc C and repeat Rows 14 and 15.

FINISHING

	Continuing to use cc C, cast off all stitches loosely, maintaining the Slip Stitch pattern.
	Using a large-eye yarn needle, weave in all ends.
	Follow the general approach for fringe shown on page 17. You will need two 21" lengths of yarn for each section of fringe. Make four sections each of white, olive, dark purple, and lavender, and two each of dark orange and light orange.
	Attach the fringe at each end, lining up each section of fringe with the corresponding color.

Another Yarn to Try

Montera by Classic Elite, 50% llama/50% wool, 3.5 oz/127 yd skeins, #3805 and #3829

Mohair and Lace

Using an intricate stitch for a border gives you lots of drama in a short amount of time. Although this border stitch can be used as an "all over" pattern on a scarf, working it at the beginning and end of the scarf makes this unique pattern stand out even more. A simple eyelet stitch is used in the middle. The border pattern may take a little time to master, but once you get used to moving the stitches from one needle to the other, it will become second nature — and well worth it.

Finished measurements

7½" x 62"

Yarn

Aristocrat by Heirloom, 50% mohair/
50% wool, 1.75 oz (50g)/83 yd (76m) balls
    3 balls #326 (light teal)

Needles

One pair US #11 (8mm) straight needles, *or
    size you need to obtain gauge*

Gauge

12 sts = 4" in Open Stitch pattern (see page
    52). *Please take time to check your gauge.*

Other supplies

Large-eye yarn needle for weaving in ends

K2tog = knit 2 stitches together

Pattern Stitches

Border Stitch (multiple of 8 stitches)

Rows 1–4: Knit to end of row.

Row 5: Knit 1; *insert needle into next stitch and wrap yarn 4 times around the point of the needle, then knit the stitch bringing all the wraps through the stitch; repeat from * to end of row.

Row 6: *Holding the yarn at the back of the work, slip 8 stitches, dropping all the extra wraps. This allows 8 long stitches to form on the right needle. Insert the left needle into the first 4 of the 8 long stitches and pass them over the second 4. Return all stitches to the left needle and knit the 8 crossed stitches in the new order. Repeat from * to end of row.

Row 7–10: Knit to end of row.

Row 11: Repeat Row 5.

Row 12: Holding yarn at back of work, slip 4 stitches, letting the extra wraps drop. Cross 2 over 2 as in Row 6 and then knit these 4 stitches. *Holding yarn at back of work, slip 8 stitches, dropping all the extra wraps. Cross 4 over 4 as in Row 6 and knit these 8 stitches. Repeat from * one more time. Slip 4 stitches, dropping the extra wraps, then cross 2 over 2 as in Row 6 and knit these 4 stitches.

Border Stitch (Rows 1–6)

Open Stitch (odd number of stitches)

Row 1–4: Knit to end of row.

Row 5: Knit 1; *yarn over, K2tog; repeat from * to end of row.

Open Stitch

KNITTING THE BORDER	
SET UP	Cast on 24 stitches.
Rows 1–12	Work Border Stitch pattern, shown on page 52.
Rows 13–22	Repeat Rows 1–10 of Border Stitch pattern. In Row 10, decrease 3 stitches, evenly spaced across the row.
KNITTING THE SCARF	
Rows 1–5	Work Open Stitch pattern as shown on page 52.
Next Rows	Continue to work Open Stitch pattern until scarf measures 57". Finish by completing Row 5 of Open Stitch pattern.
KNITTING THE BORDER	
Row 1	Work Row 1 of Border Stitch pattern, increasing 3 stitches, evenly spaced across the row.
Rows 2–12	Work Rows 2–12 of Border Stitch pattern, shown on page 52.
Rows 13–22	Repeat Rows 1–10 of Border Stitch pattern.
FINISHING	
	Cast off all stitches loosely. With large-eye yarn needle, weave in all loose ends.

Another Yarn to Try

Tartelette by Knit One Crochet Too, 50% cotton/40% tactel nylon/10% nylon, 1.75 oz/ 75 yd skeins, Pink Grapefruit/#211

Ribbon Drop Stitch

Ribbon yarns are so beautiful to look at and this Drop Stitch pattern really shows them off. It's probably not the warmest scarf you'll own, but it's certainly one that will add glamour to your wardrobe. You might want to think of it as just a long silky necklace. Drop stitches have a certain rhythm to them that makes them easier than they look. I always love projects that make it look like I've worked really hard when I haven't at all.

Finished measurements

4" x 72"

Yarn

Tartelette by Knit One Crochet Too, 50% cotton/40% tactel nylon/10% nylon, 1.75 oz (50g)/75 yd (68m) skeins

    2 skeins Velvet Rose/#253

Needles

One pair US #10½ (6.5mm) straight needles, *or size you need to obtain gauge*

Gauge

14 stitches = 4" in Drop Stitch pattern (see page 56). *Please take time to check your gauge.*

Other supplies

Large-eye yarn needle for weaving in ends

	KNITTING THE SCARF
NOTE	This scarf is worked entirely in Drop Stitch pattern, a five-row repeat. See below for instructions on how to make a "yarn over" (YO).
SET UP	Cast on 17 stitches.
Rows 1–3	Knit to end of each row.
Row 4	*Knit 1, yarn over twice; repeat from * to last stitch; knit 1.
Row 5	*Knit 1, drop both yarn overs; repeat from * to last stitch; knit 1.
Next Rows	Repeat Rows 1–5 until scarf measures 71", or desired length.
Next Rows	Knit 3 more rows.
	FINISHING
	Cast off all stitches loosely. With large-eye yarn needle, weave in all loose ends.

Handling Yarn Overs

Here are the techniques that you'll be using for the yarn overs in Rows 4 and 5.

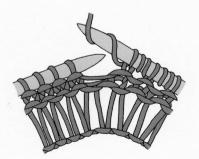

Row 4: Yarn over twice

Row 5: Drop both yarn overs

Other Yarns to Try

Swatch 1

Macaroon by TLC, 100% polyester, 3 oz/115 yd skeins, Coconut/#9316

Swatch 2

Suede by Berroco, 100% nylon, 1.75 oz/120 yd balls, Hopalong Cassidy/#3714

Swatch 3

Trendsetter Yarns by Dune, 41% mohair/30% acrylic/12% viscose/11% nylon/6% metal, 1.75 oz/90 yd balls, #94

Traveling Vine Lace

This is an old standard pattern, originally found in Barbara Walker's book *A Treasury of Knitting Patterns*, that is worked in an updated color and yarn. Mohair makes this scarf light and soft while the all-over lace pattern gives it an airy elegance. I won't lie to you, though — this pattern can be a challenge. There are lots of abbreviations and you will be subtracting and adding stitches as you work along. Don't let that intimidate you, though, because I know you're ready for this.

Finished measurements

7½" x 44"

Yarn

La Gran by Classic Elite, 76.5% mohair/ 17.5% wool/6% nylon, 1.75 oz (50g)/90 yd (83m) balls

2 balls #6519 (pink)

Needles

One pair US #10½ (6.5mm) straight needles, *or size you need to obtain gauge*

Gauge

15 stitches = 4" in Traveling Vine Stitch pattern (see page 60). *Please take time to check your gauge.*

Other supplies

Large-eye yarn needle for weaving in ends

K2tog = knit 2 together ◆ **psso** = pass slipped stitch over knit stitch ◆ **P2tog** = purl 2 together ◆ **YO** = yarn over

---

NOTE	This scarf is knit entirely in Traveling Vine Stitch pattern, which has a 12-row repeat. See Working through Back Loops on facing page for advice.
SET UP	Cast on 28 stitches.
Row 1	Knit 2; *YO, knit 1 through back loop, YO, slip 1, knit 1, psso, knit 5; repeat from * until 2 stitches remain, knit 2.
Row 2	Knit 2; *purl 4, P2tog through back loop, purl 3; repeat from * until 2 stitches remain; knit 2.
Row 3	Knit 2; *YO, knit 1 through back loop, YO, knit 2, slip 1, knit 1, psso, knit 3; repeat from * until 2 stitches remain; knit 2.
Row 4	Knit 2; *purl 2, P2tog through back loop, purl 5; repeat from * until 2 stitches remain; knit 2.
Row 5	Knit 2; *knit 1 through back loop, YO, knit 4, slip 1, knit 1, psso, knit 1, YO; repeat from * until 2 stitches remain; knit 2.
Row 6	Knit 2; *purl 1, P2tog through back loop, purl 6; repeat from * until 2 stitches remain; knit 2.

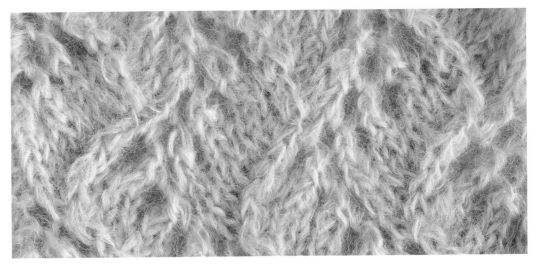

Close-up of the 12-row repeat for Traveling Vine Lace

Row 7	Knit 2; *knit 5, K2tog, YO, knit 1 through back loop, YO; repeat from * until 2 stitches remain; knit 2.
Row 8	Knit 2; *purl 3, P2tog, purl 4; repeat from * until 2 stitches remain; knit 2.
Row 9	Knit 2; *knit 3, K2tog, knit 2, YO, knit 1 through back loop, YO; repeat from * until 2 stitches remain; knit 2.
Row 10	Knit 2; *purl 5, P2tog, purl 2; repeat from * until 2 stitches remain; knit 2.
Row 11	Knit 2; *YO, knit 1, K2tog, knit 4, YO, knit 1 through back loop; repeat from * until 2 stitches remain; knit 2.
Row 12	Knit 2; *purl 6, P2tog, purl 1; repeat from * until 2 stitches remain; knit 2.
Next Rows	Repeat Rows 1–12 until scarf measures 44", or desired length.
FINISHING	
	Cast off all stitches loosely with a knit stitch.
	With large-eye yarn needle, weave in ends.

Working through Back Loops

To get the proper twist to the stitches and obtain the open-lace look that character-izes this pretty pattern, it's important to work the stitches as follows:

Odd-numbered rows:
Knit 1 through back loop

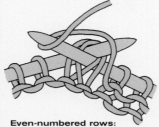

Even-numbered rows:
P2tog through back loop

Feather and Fan

The Feather and Fan is a very traditional pattern and for many years was used only for afghans. But lately this old standby has been showing up in very fashionable sweaters on runways in Milan. Chenille yarn and a modern color allow this classic pattern to come into its own in the 21st century. Although the pattern may seem difficult at first glance, it is a very simple repeat of just 4 rows.

Finished measurements
6" x 66"

Yarn
Bulky Rayon Chenille by Blue Heron Yarns, 100% rayon, 8 oz (228g)/275 yd (247m) skeins
    1 skein Clay

Needles
One pair US #10½ (6.5mm) straight needles, *or size you need to obtain gauge*

Gauge
16 stitches = 4" in Feather and Fan Stitch pattern (see page 64). *Please take time to check your gauge.*

Other supplies
Large-eye yarn needle for weaving in ends

K2tog = knit 2 together ◆ **YO** = yarn over

KNITTING THE SCARF	
NOTE	This scarf is knit entirely in Feather and Fan Stitch pattern, a 4-row repeat. Parentheses are used around short sets of instructions that fall within a longer line of instructions that are also repeated. In cases where only one set of directions is repeated, an asterik and a semicolon are used.
SET UP	Cast on 24 stitches loosely.
Row 1	Knit to end of row.
Row 2	Purl to end of row.
Row 3	*K2tog twice, (YO, knit 1) 4 times, K2tog twice; repeat from * once more.
Row 4	Knit to end of row.
Next Rows	Repeat Rows 1–4 until scarf measure 66", or desired length.
FINISHING	
	Cast off all stitches loosely. This is particularly important with chenille, as it tends to curl if it is bound off too tightly. Use a large-eye yarn needle to weave in all loose ends.

Tips for the Handling and Care of Chenille

Rather than being spun, like most yarns, chenille consists of woven fabric that has been cut lengthwise into very narrow strips. These strips tend to unravel slightly, giving the yarn its fuzzy texture. Unfortunately, this yarn structure tends to "worm." (The worms are the small loops of yarn that you'll see occasionally pop out of the fabric surface.) Getting the tension right helps avoid this tendency, but some yarns worm no matter how you handle them. In my experience, if you work a pattern stitch, rather than plain stockinette stitch, the fabric is more likely to stay put.

To avoid loops along the cast-on edge, use the knitted cast-on method, instead of the long tail cast on.

Refer to the label on the yarn for advice about care. Some acrylic chenille yarns require hand washing, whereas some rayon chenilles do *better* if laundered by machine. It's always safest to go with what the yarn manufacturer recommends.

Other Yarns to Try

Swatch 1: Kureyon by Noro, 100% wool, 1.6oz/110 yd balls, #102

Swatch 2: Cotton Classic by Tahki/Stacy Charles, 100% mercerized cotton, 1.75 oz/108 yd balls, #3476

Swatch 3: Star by Classic Elite, 99% cotton/1% Lycra, 1.6oz/112 yd balls, #5127

Woven Knit

The random colors of this yarn add to the illusion of its being woven, but it is actually knitted. Working the slip stitch with the yarn moving from front to back creates a texture that mimics a woven fabric. It also allows the scarf to remain perfectly flat. As with most Slip Stitch patterns, you will be working on a much larger needle than the yarn might call for and the rows will tend to become compressed.

Finished measurements

5¼" x 70"

Yarn

Prism by Colinette, 68% cotton/32% wool, 3½ oz (100g)/125 yd (115m) skeins

    2 skeins Toscana/#55

Needles

One pair US #11 (8mm) straight needles, *or size you need to obtain gauge*

Gauge

18 stitches = 4" in Slip Stitch pattern. *Please take time to check your gauge.*

Other supplies

Large-eye yarn needle for weaving in ends

NOTE	Throughout this pattern, you slip every other stitch on both knit and purl rows. As the pattern directs, be sure to hold the yarn in front of the slipped stitch on knit rows and in back of the stitch on purl rows (see illustration below). On knit rows, insert the needle into the stitch you are slipping in the same way you would if you were purling it; on purl rows, you also insert the needle as if to purl (which is natural). (See illustration, page 48.)
SET UP	Cast on 26 stitches. Rows 1 and 2 below comprise the Slipped Stitch pattern, which is worked throughout.
Row 1	*Knit 1, move yarn to front and slip the next stitch purlwise, move yarn back; repeat from * to end of row.
Row 2	*Purl 1, move yarn to the back and slip the next stitch purlwise, move yarn to the front; repeat from * to end of row.

Woven Stitch Techniques

To get the proper effect, it's important that you always carry the yarn on the right side of the scarf when you're slipping stitches.

Row 1 and all odd-numbered rows

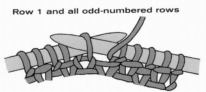

Move yarn to front and slip the next stitch as if to purl.

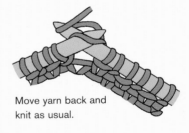

Move yarn back and knit as usual.

Row 2 and all even-numbered rows

Move yarn to back and slip the next stitch.

Move yarn to front and purl as usual.

	Repeat Rows 1 and 2 until piece measures 70", or desired length.
	Cast off all stitches loosely.
	FINISHING
	Weave in all ends.
	To make fringe, cut 20 lengths of yarn 17" long. Following the technique described on page 17, make each fringe using two strands of yarn. Attach five fringe, evenly spaced, to each end of the scarf.

Other Yarns to Try

Lamb's Pride Worsted by Brown Sheep Company, 85% wool/15% mohair, 4 oz/190 yd skeins, Brite Blue/M-57

Manos del Uruguay, 100% wool, 3.5 oz/138 yd skeins, #106
(Work two rows of one color, then two rows of the other.)

Fair Isle Favorite

Fair Isle knitting traditionally refers to knitting with many colors, and this scarf is no exception. Our updated version is worked in bright colors on a creamy background that make the motifs really stand out. The border is worked in a traditional 1 x 1 color change that fills in for fringe. If you haven't yet tried multicolor knitting, this is a good beginner project for you.

Finished measurements

6½" x 72"

Yarn

Classic Merino Wool by Patons, 100% wool,
3.5 oz (100g)/223 yd (205m) balls

mc = 1 ball Aran/#202

cc A = 1 ball Dusky Blue/#214

cc B = 1 ball Leaf Green/#240

cc C = 1 ball Magenta/#211

Needles

One pair US #9 (5.5mm) straight needles,
or size you need to obtain gauge

Gauge

18 stitches = 4" and 20 rows = 4" in Fair Isle
Stitch pattern (see page 72). *Please take
time to check your gauge.*

Other supplies

Large-eye yarn needle for weaving in ends

KNITTING THE SCARF

NOTE	The stitch pattern chart is on page 74. Follow Fair Isle Chart starting at the bottom right and working from right to left on right-side rows and from left to right on wrong-side rows. The chart is color-coded for the first color combination, but the contrasting colors change in sequence throughout, so follow the row-by-row instructions below for the sequence.

KNITTING THE BORDER

SET UP	With US #9 (5.5mm) needles, use mc to cast on 30 stitches.
Rows 1–7	Using mc and cc B, work lines 1–7 on the chart (Border).
Rows 8–14	Using mc and cc A, work lines 8–14 on the chart (Border).

KNITTING THE FAIR ISLE PATTERN

Rows 1–22	Using mc and cc C, work lines 15–36 on the chart (Star).
Rows 23–33	Using mc and cc A, work lines 37–47 on the chart (X's and O's).
Rows 34–55	Using mc and cc B, work lines 15–36 (Star).
Rows 56–66	Using mc and cc C, work lines 37–47 (X's and O's).
Rows 67–88	Using mc and cc A, work lines 15–36 (Star).
Rows 89–99	Using mc and cc B, work lines 37–47 (X's and O's).
Rows 100–121	Using mc and cc C, work lines 15–36 (Star).
Next Rows	Repeat Rows 1–121 twice more.

KNITTING THE BORDER

Rows 1–7	Using mc and cc A, work lines 8–14 on the chart (Border).
Rows 8–14	Using mc and cc B, work lines 1–7 on the chart (Border).

	FINISHING	
		Cast off all stitches loosely.
		Use a large-eye yarn needle to weave in all loose ends.
		Since this scarf is worked in stockinette stitch, it will have a tendency to roll. In this case, that can be a good thing. The wrong side, which is clearly the inside on Fair Isle, doesn't show.

The Joy of Color

You can create an infinite number of fascinating designs by knitting with two or more colors in a single row or round. The multicolor knitting in this book is called Fair Isle (or stranded) knitting, in which two (or more) colors interchange regularly all the way across the row.

When you change color within a row, always take the color you want to emphasize from below the other. On the front, the color handled this way will dominate the pattern and create a more uniform design. Be sure to be consistent and take the same yarn over and the other under throughout the project.

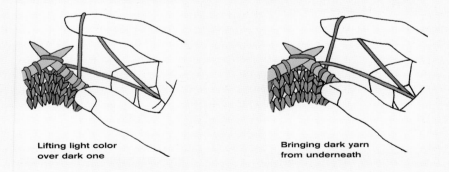

Lifting light color over dark one

Bringing dark yarn from underneath

When you knit with more than one color, carry the other color or colors along the wrong side. Keep the carried yarn loose and don't carry it for more than three stitches. For wider runs in the pattern, catch the carried yarn by wrapping the working yarn from beneath and around it every three or four stitches.

FAIR ISLE CHART

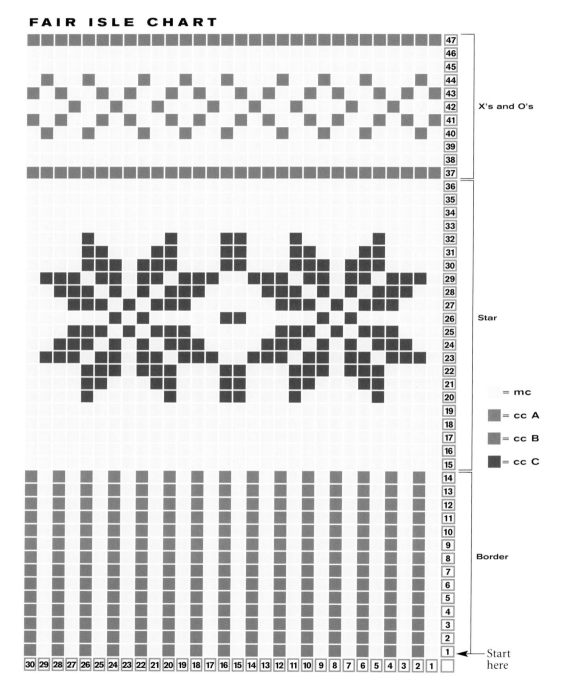

47
46
45
44
43
42
41
40
39
38
37

X's and O's

36
35
34
33
32
31
30
29
28
27
26
25
24
23
22
21
20
19
18
17
16
15

Star

☐ = mc

▨ = cc A

▨ = cc B

■ = cc C

14
13
12
11
10
9
8
7
6
5
4
3
2
1

Border

← Start here

30 29 28 27 26 25 24 23 22 21 20 19 18 17 16 15 14 13 12 11 10 9 8 7 6 5 4 3 2 1

Other Yarns to Try

■ **mc**

Lamb's Pride Worsted by Brown Sheep Company, 85% wool/15% mohair, 4 oz/190 yd skeins, Rust/M-97

■ **cc A**

Lamb's Pride Worsted by Brown Sheep Company, 85% wool/15% mohair, 4 oz/190 yd skeins, Brite Blue/M-57

■ **cc B**

Lamb's Pride Worsted by Brown Sheep Company, 85% wool/15% mohair, 4 oz/ 190 yd skeins, Ponderosa Pine/M-27

■ **cc C**

Prairie Silk by Brown Sheep Company, 72% wool/18% mohair/10% silk, 1.75 oz/88 yd skeins, Ruble Red/#PS400

Snuggly Neck Warmer

A scarf with a hole in it! That may sound strange, but the hole serves a very important purpose. Just pull one end of the scarf through the hole and you will be able to tighten up the scarf around your neck so that it will stay neatly in place. It is worked in a soft, snuggly yarn that will chase away the winter blues.

Finished measurements

10" x 48"

Yarns

Plush by Berroco, 100% nylon, 1.75 oz (50g)/
90 yd (82m) balls

    3 balls Crema/#1901

Needles

US #13 (9mm) straight needles, *or size you
need to obtain gauge*

Gauge

8 stitches = 4" in garter stitch (knit every row).
    Please take time to check your gauge.

Other supplies

Large-eye yarn needle for weaving in ends,
    stitch holder

	KNITTING THE SCARF
Set Up	Cast on 22 stitches.
Row 1	Knit to end of row.
	Repeat Row 1 (garter stitch) until piece measures 31".
	MAKING THE SLIT
Row 1	Knit 11 stitches, then slip the remaining 11 stitches onto a stitch holder.
Row 2	Working on just the first 11 stitches, knit each row until piece measures 33". Cut yarn, leaving a 6" tail for weaving in.
Next Rows	Slip the 11 stitches on the holder to a needle and put the 11 stitches you have just worked onto the stitch holder. Join yarn, leaving a 6" tail for weaving in. Work on these 11 stitches, knitting each row as before, until the new section has the same number of rows as the first section.
Next Row	Place the stitches on the holder on the empty needle and join the two sections by knitting across those 11 stitches.
	FINISHING THE SCARF
	Continue to work in garter stitch until piece measures 48".
	Cast off all stitches loosely.
	With a large-eye yarn needle, weave in any loose ends.

Other Yarns to Try

Swatch 1: Pastaza by Cascade Yarns, 50% llama/50% wool, 3.5 oz/132 yd skeins, #1107

Swatch 2: Divine by Patons, 80% acrylic/18% mohair/2% polyester, 3.5 oz/142 yd balls, Denim Storm/#06117

Swatch 3: Quest by Berroco, 100% nylon, 1.75 oz/82 yd skeins, Bronze/#9811

Random Diagonals

The beauty of this basically garter stitch scarf is that it is entirely your own creation. The interesting diagonal pattern is amazingly simple: Every other row, you do a yarn over at the beginning of the row, then knit two stitches together at the end. Use the yarns suggested, or experiment with bold colors and/or novelty yarns.

Finished measurements

4" x 60"

Yarns

Amore by Coats & Clark, 80% acrylic/ 20% nylon, 6 oz (170g)/290 yd (265m) skeins
  1 skein #3625 (celery)
  1 skein #3534 (plum)

La Gran by Classic Elite, 76.5% mohair/17.5% wool/6% nylon, 1.75 oz (50g)/90 yd (83m) balls
  1 ball #6562 (dark teal)
  1 ball # 6509 (light teal)

Montera by Classic Elite, 50% llama/50% wool, 1.75 oz (50g)/127 yd (116m) skeins
  1 skein #3826 (dark purple)
  1 skein #3832 (citron)

'03 Tweed by Classic Elite, 65% wool/ 20% nylon/15% acrylic, 1.75oz (50g)/143 yd (131m) skeins
  1 skein #5957 (aqua)

Cotton Chenille by Crystal Palace Yarns, 100% cotton, 1.6 oz (50g)/98 yd (90m) cones
  1 cone #1404 (light purple)

Needles

One pair US #9 (5.5mm) straight needles, *or size you need to obtain gauge*

Gauge

14 stitches = 4", 28 rows = 4" in garter stitch. *Please take time to check your gauge.*

Other supplies

Large-eye yarn needle for weaving in ends

	KNITTING THE SCARF
NOTE	Rows 1 and 2 are the Pattern Stitch. Continue to work in this Pattern Stitch throughout the scarf, while at the same time changing colors to create the stripes (see At Random, below). You'll find it's helpful to weave in your color change ends as you work.
SET UP	Using Amore celery, cast on 20 stitches.
Row 1	Knit 1, yarn over, knit 16, knit 2 together, knit 1.
Row 2	Knit to end of row, *knitting into the back of each yarn over as you come to it.*
Next Rows	Repeat Rows 1 and 2 until the piece measures 60", or desired length.
	FINISHING
	Cast off all stitches loosely.
	With a large-eye yarn needle, weave in all loose ends.

At Random

The spontaneous fun that characterizes this scarf is the result of random color changes. Start new yarns in the middle of rows, staggering the changeovers throughout so that you end up with an uneven effect. I used the following color sequence:

Amore celery	La Gran light teal
Montera citron	Cotton Chenille
La Gran dark teal	Amore plum
'03 Tweed aqua	Montera dark purple

Because the rows are knit at a diagonal, the scarf is not as wide as one might expect. I was actually a little surprised to see how narrow the scarf was when I finished. If you want a wider scarf, just cast on more stitches.

Other Yarns to Try

Swatch 1: Cascade Yarns 220, 100% wool, 3.5 oz/220 yd skeins, #7830 and #7824; Victorian Brushed Mohair by Halcyon Yarn, 70% mohair/24% wool/ 6% nylon, 14 oz/145 yd mini-skeins, #118; Matchmaker by Jaeger, 100% merino wool, 1.75 oz/131 yd balls, #887; Botanica by Halcyon Yarn, 100% wool, 4 oz/160 yd skeins, #23; Flutter by KFI, 100% polyester, .71 oz/75 yd balls, #25; 1824 Wool by Mission Falls, 100% merino superwash wool, 1.75 oz/ 85 yd balls, #25; Zen by Berroco, 40% cotton/60% nylon, 1.75 oz/110 yd skeins, #8223; Sparkle and Gleam Chainette by Halcyon Yarn, lurex/rayon, 1.5 oz/200 yd mini-cones, #2

Swatch 2: Lopi by Reynolds, 100% virgin wool, 3.5 oz/110 yd balls, #0170

Swatch 3: Lamb's Pride Superwash (worsted) by Brown Sheep Co, 100% washable wool, 3.5 oz/110 yd skeins, Alabaster/#SW10; Sparkle and Gleam Chainette by Halcyon Yarn, lurex/rayon, 1.5 oz/200 yd mini-cones, #2; Fizz by Crystal Palace, 100% polyester, 1.75 oz/120 yd balls, Sage Mix/#9154; Mohair by Colinette, 78% mohair/13% wool/9% nylon, 3.2 oz/191 yd skeins, Moss; Quest by Berroco, 100% nylon, 1.75 oz/82 yd hanks, Marilyn Pink/#9831; Jewel FX by Berroco, 94% rayon/6% metallic, .875 oz/57 yd balls, Rhinestones/#6907; Imagine by Classic Elite, 53% cotton/47% rayon, 1.75 oz/93 yd skeins, Meadow/#9211; Posh by Classic Elite, 30% cashmere/70% silk, 1.75 oz/125 yd balls, Hydrangea/#PSH93051

Mohair Diamonds

With its zigzag edges and chevronlike patterning, this playful scarf is as much fun to wear as it is to make. This is modular knitting at its most delightful. Each small square begins with only 15 stitches. Steep decreases at the center of every other row quickly reduce the number of stitches to 1, creating a small square. Once you get the rhythm of the pattern, you won't want to stop.

Finished measurements

8" x 45"

Yarn

Mohair Classic Heathers from Halcyon Yarn
78% mohair/13% wool/9% nylon, 1.5 oz
(43g)/90 yd (82m) mini-cones

   cc A = 1 mini-cone #6 (blue)

   cc B = 1 mini-cone #19 (white)

   cc C = 1 mini-cone #1 (gray)

Needles

One pair US #5 (3.75 mm) straight needles,
   10" long (see Shorties, page 89), *or size
   you need to obtain gauge*

Gauge

Each pattern square = 2" x 2". *Please take time
   to check your gauge.*

Other supplies

Large-eye yarn needle for weaving in ends

---

cc = contrasting color ◆ **K2tog** = knit
2 together ◆ **mc** = main color ◆
psso = pass slipped stitch over knit
stitch

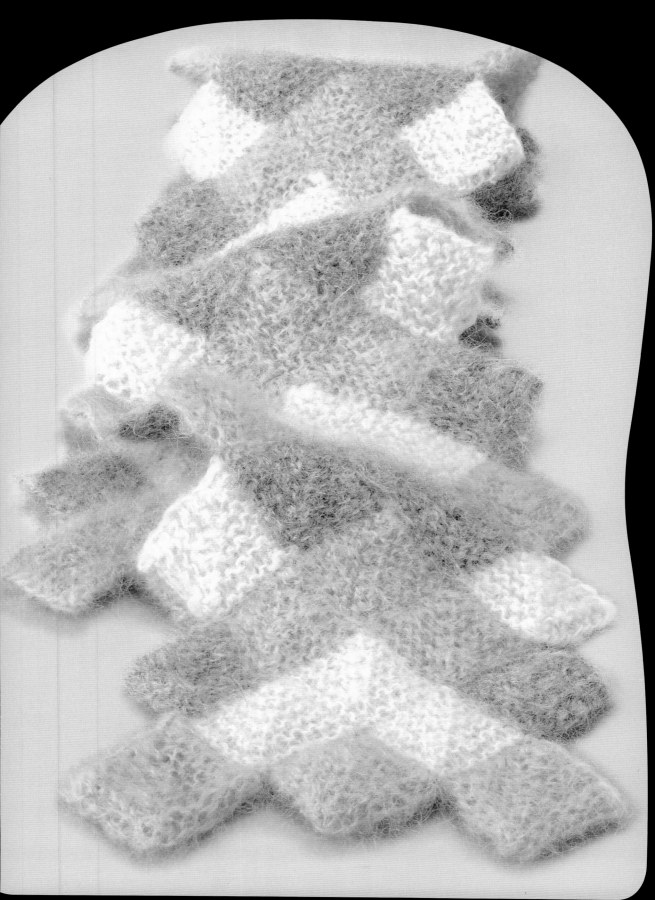

KNITTING THE BASIC SQUARE

NOTE	Since this scarf is knit modularly in a series of small squares, we're presenting the directions in a slightly different format from that for the rest of the projects. The basic technique is the same for all squares, but there are variations for the squares on each side edge, as well as another variation for the starting edge. Begin by working three basic squares, which will form the bottom edge.
	All decreases are made on right-side rows. See On the Decrease, below, for technique for K2tog and psso.
SET UP	Using cc A, cast on 15 stitches.
Row 1	Knit to end of row.
Row 2	Slip 1, knit 5, slip 1, K2tog, psso, knit 5, purl 1. You now have 13 stitches.
Rows 3, 5, 7, 9, 11, 13	Slip 1, knit to last stitch, purl 1.

On the Decrease

This pattern requires two simple decrease stitches to be worked one after the other: slip 1 stitch, knit 2 together (K2tog), then pass the slipped stitch over the knit stitch (psso). This sequence creates a sharp decrease that not only determines the shape of each square, but also provides an interesting decorative feature running diagonally up the square. The decrease line runs from bottom to top corners, not side to side. The pattern provides guidance to help you maintain this feature.

Psso is a common method of decreasing that is usually accomplished by working just one stitch following the slipped stitch; in this pattern, it's worked as follows: Slip one stitch from the left needle to the right, inserting the needle as if to knit the stitch but without knitting it. Knit the next two stitches together **(K2tog)** by inserting the needle into both loops, as you would to knit, then use the left needle to draw the slipped stitch over the just-knitted stitch.

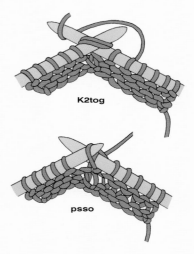

K2tog

psso

Row 4	Slip 1, knit 4, slip 1, K2tog, psso, knit 4, purl 1. You now have 11 stitches.
Row 6	Slip 1, knit 3, slip 1, K2tog, psso, knit 3, purl 1. You now have 9 stitches.
Row 8	Slip 1, knit 2, slip 1, K2tog, psso, knit 2, purl 1. You now have 7 stitches.
Row 10	Slip 1 knit 1, slip 1, K2tog, psso, knit 1, purl 1. You now have 5 stitches.
Row 12	Slip 2, K2tog, psso, purl 1. You now have 3 stitches.
Row 14	Slip 1, K2tog, psso.
	Cut yarn, leaving a 3" tail, and draw the tail through the final stitch.
	Using cc A, knit two more squares exactly like the first. You have now completed Squares #1, 2, and 3 (see layout, page 90).

(see layout, page 90)

JOINING THE BOTTOM SQUARES

Set Up	Place two of the squares side by side with corners touching and with the decrease line running vertically from the bottom corner to the top.

Heads & Tails

beginning tail

ending tail

One diamond

If you keep this orientation in mind, you'll find it's easier to stay on track while making this scarf: The tail for the cast-on is always at the right when you're working on the right side of the scarf. The tail remaining from the last stitch is always at the top. The line that marks the decreases and runs from bottom to top corners should be vertical throughout the scarf.

	Using cc B, pick up and knit 8 stitches along the top left edge of the right-hand square. (**NOTE:** Be sure to go under both loops of the edge stitches. Because of the way you work the first and last stitches of each row, these should be easy to locate.)
	Continuing on the same needle, pick up 7 stitches along the top right edge of the left-hand square. You now have 15 stitches.
	Repeat Rows 1–14 under Knitting the Basic Square. You have now completed Square #4.
	Place the remaining unattached square (Square #3) at the right of the joined pair, lining it up so that its left corner touches the right corner of Square #2 and the decrease line runs vertically from the bottom corner to the top.
	Using cc B, pick up 8 stitches along the top left edge of Square #3, then pick up 7 stitches along the top right edge of Square #2. You now have 15 stitches. Repeat Rows 1–14 under Knitting the Basic Square. You have now completed Square #5 and have five attached squares.
KNITTING A RIGHT-EDGE SQUARE	
SET UP	Using cc C, cast on 7 stitches.

At Loose Ends

Once you get in the swing of how to attach each new "diamond" to the preceding one, this pattern is fairly easy. It does result in quite a few tails, however, since you start with a new piece of yarn for each new diamond. You'll thank yourself heartily, therefore, if you weave in the loose ends as you knit, rather than waiting until the whole scarf is finished to tackle the job. Take whatever tails are available at the point where you begin a new diamond and weave them in and out of the working yarn as you knit the first five or six stitches of the row. You can do this only when you're working right-side rows, so there will still be a few out-of-reach tails left over when you complete the scarf, but these can be threaded through a large-eye needle and quickly taken care of. Be sure to weave in all tails along the line of adjacent squares, where they'll be less visible. The wrong side of the scarf does show seams, but if you weave in the tails neatly, they are not unattractive.

	Continuing on the same needle, pick up 8 stitches along the top right edge of Square #5 (refer to Diamonds Chart on page 90). You now have 15 stitches.
	Repeat Rows 1–14 under Knitting the Basic Square.

Set Up	Using cc C, pick up 8 stitches along the top left edge of Square #4.
	Turn your needle and, continuing at the same point, cast on 7 stitches. You now have 15 stitches.
	Repeat Rows 1–14 under Knitting the Basic Square.

KNITTING A MIDDLE SQUARE

Set Up	Using cc B, pick up 7 stitches along the top left edge of Square #5, pick up 1 stitch at the point where the three corners come together, then pick up 7 stitches along the top right edge of Square #4. You now have 15 stitches.
	Repeat Rows 1–14 under Knitting the Basic Square.

KNITTING THE SCARF

	Follow the Mohair Diamond Scarf Layout on page 90 for color sequences to complete the scarf.

Shorties

In this pattern, you never work with more than 15 stitches on your needles at any one time, and you decrease rapidly, eliminating 2 stitches every other row. Because you use so few stitches and turn the needles so frequently, you'll find that it's much easier to use short needles. If you have US #5 double-point needles in your knitting bag, you may even want to make your own pair of shorties for this project. Just put a needle protector on one end of each needle to keep the stitches from falling off, then use them as you would any straight needles.

MOHAIR DIAMOND SCARF LAYOUT

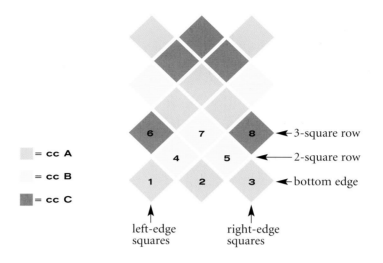

= cc A

= cc B

= cc C

3-square row

2-square row

bottom edge

left-edge squares

right-edge squares

Tips for Success

• Think of the structure of this scarf as alternating rows of two and three squares. For example, Squares #4 and #5 comprise a two-square row and Squares #6, #7, and #8 comprise a three-square row. You'll find that it's less confusing if you complete an entire three-square row before working the next two-square row. Use the instructions for Knitting a Right-Edge Square (pages 88–89) for all squares along the right edge, which are attached to other squares only on their top and bottom left sides. Similarly, use the instructions for Knitting a Left-Edge Square (page 89) for all squares along the left edge, which are attached only on their top and bottom right sides.

• Make sure that your diagonal line of decreases always runs from bottom to top throughout the scarf.

• When picking up stitches to start a new square, take special care at the point where four corners converge, so that you maintain nice sharp corners.

• Weave in as many loose ends as possible as you work the scarf.

Glossary

ASTERISK (*): Repeat directions contained between asterisks, often across the row. For example, if you have 12 stitches and the directions say, "*Knit 2, knit 2 together; repeat from * to end of row," you will work the sequence "knit 2, knit 2 together" three times.

BLOCKING: You can use several techniques to prevent a scarf from rolling. For wool, you can pin the scarf to the size you want and hold a steam iron over it. Or wet a towel, lay it over the scarf, and then very lightly touch an iron to the wet towel, just enough to release steam into the wool. Never press down or move the iron back and forth or you'll flatten and distort the stitches. For wool blends, mohair, angora, alpaca, or cashmere, just slightly dampen the surface and pin it to a flat surface where it can air dry.

CAST OFF: Casting off (sometimes called binding off) is a technique for taking the stitches off the needle so that the knitting does not unravel. Here's a general-purpose cast-off: Knit two stitches, then draw the first stitch over the second and slip it off the needle. Knit the next stitch and draw the second stitch over it. Repeat until all stitches are bound off. Cut the tail of yarn, thread it through the remaining stitch, and tighten it.

CAST ON: The long-tail cast on makes a neat, firm but elastic edge: Estimate length of "tail" by wrapping yarn around needle one time for each cast-on stitch you need. Make a slip knot right here and slide knot over a knitting needle. Hold needle in your right hand; hold tail over thumb and working end of yarn over index finger of your left hand. Insert needle under front loop of tail on your thumb. Bring needle over and behind working yarn on index finger. Use needle to draw working yarn through loop on your thumb; release loop. Place thumb under tail and draw yarns toward you, holding both firmly.

CIRCULAR NEEDLES: These can be used for either flat or circular knitting. Circular needles consist of a pair of short straight needles joined by a flexible nylon or plastic center cord. In order to get a comfortable grip, choose a needle with straight ends that are long enough to span your closed hand. Also, make sure that the joint between the needle and the cord is very smooth.

DECREASE: A decrease reduces the total number of stitches. In this book, decreases are made either by knitting two stitches together (K2tog) or by slipping a stitch, knitting the next stitch, then passing the slipped stitch over the knit stitch (psso).

DOUBLE-POINTED NEEDLES: These can be used for either circular or flat knitting, but in this book they are used only for flat knitting. They consist of two needles with a rubber stop at one end.

FAIR ISLE KNITTING: Fair Isle (also known as stranded) knitting creates patterns by using more than one color in a row. Traditional patterns usually have no more than two colors in a single row. The color sequence is indicated by a chart on which each stitch is represented by a colored square. Follow the chart, line by line, beginning at the bottom right.

GARTER STITCH: This is a very simple stitch that is great for beginners: Just knit every row.

JOIN NEW YARN: When you need to change colors for stripes or Fair Isle patterns or to begin a new ball of yarn, you'll find that every knitter has a favorite way of making the join. We recommend working in the new tail on the wrong side of the piece for the last six or seven stitches before it's needed, by catching it under the working yarn. Then, when you change yarns, leave a 3-inch (7.5 cm) tail of the old yarn that you can work in in the same manner.

PARENTHESES: These function in the same way that asterisks do. They are used around short sets of directions that fall within longer lines of directions that are also repeated.

PICK UP STITCHES: Slide the point of the left needle into an existing loop. Knit that loop as a stitch.

ROW: All stitches worked once across a straight needle.

SEED STITCH: This stitch produces a nicely textured look. Working an *odd number of stitches,* knit 1, purl 1 to end of every row. You will be knitting into every knit stitch of the previous row and purling into every purl stitch of the previous row.

STITCH HOLDERS: These are used to prevent stitches from unraveling. They come in many shapes, or you can use safety pins as an alternative.

STOCKINETTE STITCH: This stitch is formed by knitting all of the stitches on the right side of the work and purling all of the stitches on the wrong side of the work.

TAIL: The excess yarn left when stitches are cast on or the excess yarn left when stitches are bound off. The tail can be used to sew openings closed. Weave in the tails on the inside of the work.

WEAVE IN ENDS: Thread the tail in a yarn needle and sew the end through a few stitches on the back of the work. Always weave along rows of stitches horizontally, taking care that the yarn doesn't show on the right side. After five or six stitches, reverse direction and weave back along the tail for two or three stitches to lock it in place. Cut off any excess tail.

YARN OVER: Wrap yarn completely around the needle before working the next stitch.

"Horseshoe" lace stitch pattern (from page 17)

Row 1: (Wrong side) Purl to end of row.

Row 2: K1, *yo, K3, slip 1, K2tog, psso, K3, yo, K1; repeat from * to end of row.

Row 3: Purl to end of row.

Row 4: P1, *K1, yo, K2, slip 1, K2tog, psso, K2, yo, K1, P1; repeat from * to end of row.

Row 5: K1, *P9, K1; repeat from * to end of row.

Row 6: P1, *K2, yo, K1, slip 1, K2tog, psso, K1, yo, K2, P1; repeat from * to end of row.

Row 7: Follow directions in Row 5.

Row 8: P1, *K3, yo, slip 1, K2tog, psso, yo, K3, P1; repeat from * to end of row.

Repeat these 8 rows for pattern.

Acknowledgments

Many thanks to

The knitters and test knitters who helped make the projects for this book:
Joyce Nordstrom for all of her excellent knitting and for never saying no when
I need a project done quickly,. Amy Hsu and Dawn Holton for making their
knitting needles "fly," and Diana Foster for test knitting all of the patterns.

My family:
My daughter, Heather, for always listening and knitting a scarf,
my husband, Tom, for making it all possible with his love and understanding,
my mom, Jean, because without her I wouldn't be so creative,
and my sister, Rajeana, for being a best friend.

The companies that supplied yarn:
Berroco, Inc. of Uxbridge, Massachusetts
Classic Elite Yarns of Lowell, Massachusetts
Halcyon Yarn of Bath, Maine

I would also like to thank Christina Stork Launer at Article Pract,
Wendy Scofield for styling the scarves for the photo shoot, and
all the wonderful people at Storey who make this process enjoyable and fun,
especially Sarah Guare and Gwen Steege — they always make me look and sound good.

Index

Page numbers for charts are in **bold**; those for photos and illustrations are in *italics*.

Other Storey Titles You Will Enjoy

Knit Baby Blankets! edited by Gwen Steege
ISBN 1-58017-495-7

Knit Baby Head & Toes! edited by Gwen Steege
ISBN 1-58017-494-9

Knit Christmas Stockings! edited by
Gwen Steege
ISBN 1-58017-505-8

Knit Hats! edited by Gwen Steege
ISBN 1-58017-482-5

Knit Mittens! by Robin Hansen
ISBN 1-58017-483-3

Knit Socks! by Betsy McCarthy
ISBN 1-58017-537-6